# AT HOME

## BARRON'S

Books in the
WATCH OUT! Series:

WATCH OUT! Around Town
WATCH OUT! At Home
WATCH OUT! Near Water
WATCH OUT! On the Road

First Edition for the United States and Canada published in 2006
by Barron's Educational Series, Inc.

Text copyright © Claire Llewellyn 2006
Illustrations copyright © Mike Gordon 2006

Published by Hodder Children's Books in 2006

All inquiries should be addressed to:
Barron's Educational Series, Inc.
250 Wireless Boulevard
Hauppauge, New York 11788
**www.barronseduc.com**

International Standard Book No. 13: 978-0-7641-3323-7
International Standard Book No. 10: 0-7641-3323-3

Library of Congress Catalog Card No. 2005926319

Printed in China
9 8 7 6 5 4 3 2 1

# WATCH OUT!

# AT HOME

Written by Claire Llewellyn

Illustrated by Mike Gordon

BARRON'S

Home is where you live with your family. It's a very special place.

4

Spot

5

Home is where you play your favorite games.

It's comfortable and safe.
Or is it?

6

Have you ever slipped on
the stairs and gone
bump
bump
bump
to the bottom?

Perhaps home is not always as safe as it seems.

Thank goodness someone's usually around to keep an eye on you.

But what if Mom's busy,
or Dad's on the phone?

Can you take care of yourself?

Some items around the house are sharp.

Some sharp items are useful for cutting things.

Sharp scissors →

Sharp knife →

Sharp saw ↓

But what could happen if you played with them?

# Many things in the house are hot.

Hot iron

Hot kettle

Hot pan

Hot cup

Hot dish

Hot oven

Hot toaster

## What would happen if you touched them?

Always be careful when you're near hot things.

Fire is another thing that's hot.

Burning flames are very pretty, but can set the house on fire.

Many things in the house
have plugs and wires.

When you plug them in
and switch them on, they begin to work.

These machines run on electricity. Electricity is a kind of power, and helps us in all sorts of ways.

But did you know electricity is dangerous?

Electrical things have different parts.

wire
← mom
← switch
Sam
vacuum
plug
socket

It's important to leave them all alone.

Never play with electrical things.

Don't touch, Teddy. It could hurt you very badly!

How do you keep your house clean?

Most of us use polish, sprays, and other cleaning products.

Household cleaners are very strong.

It's best to stay away from them.
Do you know why?

Medicines are also very strong.
A little medicine can help you
when you are sick.

But too much could make you very ill.

Medicines should always be
locked away.

Pills are dangerous, you silly bear!

Even when you're being careful, accidents sometimes happen.

If Mom or Dad is not around, who do you think could help?

friend's dad

babysitter

neighbor

big brothe

Most of the time,
your home is safe.

But keep an eye
open for danger.

And before you do something that could be risky ...

stop and ask yourself—*Is it safe?*

Then, before you know it, you'll be taking care of other people, too!

# Notes for parents and teachers

## Watch Out!

There are four titles currently in the *Watch Out!* series: *On the Road*, *Near Water*, *At Home*, and *Around Town*. These books will prompt young readers to think about safety concerns both inside and outside the home, while traveling in a car, and even while on a trip or enjoying the outdoors. The lessons illustrated in all four books will help children identify important safety issues and potentially dangerous situations that they may come across in their everyday lives. Gaining the ability to recognize potential dangers—as well as being instructed on how to avoid these hazards—will allow readers to be more aware of the world around them. Whether at home, at a park, by the pool, or on a road trip, this series offers helpful tips and information on a number of common, everyday scenarios children should *watch out* for.

## Issues raised in the book

*Watch Out! At Home* is intended to be an enjoyable book that discusses the importance of safety in the home. Throughout, children are given the opportunity to think about taking care of themselves and about what might happen if they don't. It allows them time to explore these issues and discuss them with their family, class, and school. It encourages them to think about safety first and about their own responsibility in keeping safe.

The book looks at the things at home that are potentially hazardous—knives, electricity sockets, and matches, for example—

and asks questions about the consequences of playing with dangerous things.

It is also full of situations that children and adults will have encountered. It allows a child to ask and answer questions on a one-to-one basis with you. How can you avoid accidents at home? What should you do if things go wrong? Who are the best people to help you if they do? The illustrations help to answer these questions with ideas and suggestions.

Being safe at home is important for everyone. Can your children think of an incident in which they fell down, or burned themselves on something hot? What happened? How did it feel? The book tackles these and many other issues. It uses open-ended questions to encourage children to think for themselves about the consequences of their behavior.

## Suggestions for follow-up activities

Make a model of your home and point out areas where there are potential dangers. Discuss the different types of dangers that might be encountered around the home.

Look at the labels on bottles with your child and see which ones have warning labels.

Think about all the things in the home that use electricity. Now ask your child to draw a sign that means "Warning—this is dangerous."

Stick it to electrical items around the house to highlight the potential danger.

List all the things that could be hot in your house. Discuss different ways you can avoid getting burnt.

www.safekids.org—Safe Kids is a national campaign designed to help protect kids from accidents through education. The Web site contains information about various threats to children, product recalls, and research findings.

## Books to read

Baker, Eugene H. *Home (Safety First)*. Creative Co., 1986.
Illustrated guide to children's safety in the home.

Gross, Patty Myers. *Fire Safety*. Roo Publications, 1997.
Hip Hop Mob Kangaroo teaches techniques for children to utilize in fire situations.

Millagan, Jacquie. *Spring Cleaning Household Poisons (Early Childhood Safety Series)*. T. S. Denison, 1988.
Information for children about avoiding potentially dangerous chemicals, which are common in the home.

Ramsay, Helena. *Look Out at Home*. Evans Publishing Group, 2003.